Pioneer
Free Will Baptists
Ministers
Burial Locations
In
Wisconsin

This book was printed in the United States of America.

To order additional copies of this book, contact:
FWB Publications
Enchanting Acres
1006 Rayme Drive
Columbus, Ohio 43207
Alton.loveless@prodigy.net
Or
www.amazon.com

FWB
FWB Publications

Introduction

Wisconsin

This book represents all that were part of the Free Will Baptist movement, consisting of the Palmer (south), Randall (north) and others such as the Stone, John-Thomas, John Wheeler Assns., NC OFWB and more.

Many of the photos are poor quality, but it was all I could find. Likewise, I do not have photos or tombstones for many of them. The information about these ministers were all that was available to me or found in archives. I made every effort to include those for which they would be remembered. Some I had no information, but research had shown they were of our denomination.

This Section is taken for a two Volume set done by this author.

Wisconsin

George C Alborn
Birth:
1877
Death:
1956
Burial:
Wauwatosa Cemetery
Wauwatosa,
Milwaukee County,
Wisconsin

Rev. Alborn, a graduate of Hillside College, a Free Baptist institution and the first college in Michigan to organize under the general college law in 1853, was a prolific and scholarly writer, publishing a novel (Ish Kerioth, 1904), a history (History of the First Baptist Church if Bricelin, Minnesota, 1933) and a collection of poetry (Rhythms of Life), 1941,

He served as pastor of the Burnett church (Dodge County) from 1899 to 1901, the Fairwater (Fond du Lac County) and Grand Prairie (Green Lake County) churches from 1902 to 1905, the Greenbush church (Sheboygan County) from 1906 to 1907, the Allenville church (Winnebago County) from 1908 to 1909, and the Oak Center and Oakfield churches (Fond du Lac County) in 1911. Following the dissolution of the Wisconsin Freewill Baptist church, he also served other congregations including the Underwood Memorial church in Wauwatosa.

Rev. Alborn also served as secretary of the Home Mission Board of the Wisconsin Freewill church and was instrumental in promoting the merger of the Freewill church with the general Baptist church, as reported in the May, 2007, newsletter of the historical society:

The topic of reunion remained relatively quiet until 1904, when it was raised again during Yearly Meetings in Wisconsin, Minnesota and Maine in the belief that the

Baptist church had grown closer to the theological positions of the Freewill church.

Among other initiatives, Rev. George C. Alborn, pastor of the Fairwater congregation, advanced a resolution at the Wisconsin Yearly Meeting calling for a merger of the two denominations. In response, the national General Conference created a committee to study the issue. In accordance with an act passed by the 1913 legislature authorizing the change, the trustees of the Wisconsin Yearly Meeting of Freewill Baptists, in session at Fairwater, Wis., September 23, voted to dissolve the corporation. The resolution filed with the secretary of state provides that all property coming to the corporation shall inure to the benefit of the Wisconsin Baptist state convention, and that the affairs of the corporation shall be wound

up. Rev. P. Kisner is president and Rev. George C. Alborn secretary of the convention. (September 30, 1913, Janesville Daily Gazette)

Rev Abiezer Bridges
Birth:
Feb. 5, 1786
Penobscot
Hancock County
Maine, USA
Death:
Mar. 22, 1883
Monticello, Wis
Burial:
Zwingli Cemetery
Monticello
Green County
Wisconsin

Rev. Abiezer Bridges closed his earthly pilgrimage at aged 79 years. He was converted and commenced preaching on South Fox Island, Maine, where his labors were blessed. He was at this time connected with the Congregationalists. Being a Free Baptist in sentiment, he went to Lincolnville, where he was baptized, and ordained in 1821. He preached in various places with success, organizing churches at Long Island, Hope, and China, and baptizing during his ministry more than 1,000 converts.

Without especial training for the work, his good common sense, and his happy faculty of expressing his ideas clearly and easily with his love of singing, gave him a large measure of success.

Jesse Burnham
Birth:
May 16, 1778 Lee,
Strafford County,
New Hampshire
Death:
Dec. 5, 1869
Janesville,
Rock County, Wisconsin
Burial:
Mount Pleasant Cemetery,
Rock County, Wisconsin

He moved to Sebec, Maine, in 1806, and began to preach there with success. Jointly with Rev. Mr. Sealels and Rev. Mr. Libby organized a church there. Baptized many hundreds in the region where now are the towns of Atkinson, Charlestown, Garland, Corinth, Dexter, Exeter, Bradford, Dover, Foxcroft, Sebec, Brownsville, Milo, Medford and other places and gathered them into the Sebec Quarter Meeting. He was ordained in 1808 in New Hampshire, and He moved to Maxfield, ME, 1815, and Howland, ME, 1818. Organized a church there. Afterward, organized churches at Passadumkeng, ME, another at Lincoln, and Lowell, ME. In 1840 he moved to Janesville, Wisconsin, being the second Free Will Baptist minister in WI, after Rev. Mr. Cheney, together, organized the First QM in Wisconsin. He organized Prairie du Sac church in 1841. He assisted in organizing the Honey Creek Q.M. and was also in the Yearly Meeting. He did good service as a pioneer preacher on the prairies of Wisconsin and northern Illinois. He labored many years and died in his 86th year, preaching till within four weeks of his death.

Richard M Cary
Birth:
Dec. 10, 1794
Williamsburg,
Hampshire County,
Massachusetts
Death:
Oct. 16, 1868
Rock County, Wisconsin

Burial:
North Johnstown Cemetery,
Milton,
Rock County, Wisconsin

In 1806, when still a young boy his family moved to western New York, which was rugged and wild with no neighbor south or west, for 40 miles. He had limited opportunity for education or religious training, but by untiring effort he began to study and received a common English education. No minister was near when needed for a funeral, so his father often said the words of comfort; this the father did for Richard's brother, Calvin, who was killed at Buffalo, NY in War of 1812. His brother's death affected Richard deeply. In 1814, a Freewill Baptist missionary, the Rev. Jeremiah Folsom, visited this newly settled country, and he embraced the earliest opportunity of hearing the stranger. In Sept. 1816, he was baptized with seven others and organized with them into a Freewill Baptist Church. He felt impressed with a duty to preach. On Oct. 3, 1816, Erie Co. NY, he delivered his first sermon. He was ordained in June 1820 to the ministry. He began to hold meetings and baptize a number of converts. In Nov.

he organized a church and pastored the church for a portion of the time for the next twenty years. In Aug. 1821 he assisted in the organization of the Holland Purchase Yearly Meeting, which included all twenty-seven churches. At this time, he became acquainted with David Marks, a lad of 15 years, who was out on his first preaching tour. They together, at Eden, had a large number they organized into a church. He continued in ministry until 1842 when he moved out West, to Johnstown, Wis. Where he soon organized a church. He took a leading part in planting other churches and in organizing the Wisconsin Y.M. He also pastored two years in Cherry Valley, IL in the 1850's. Elder Cary was a man of unbiased judgment and earnest convictions, with more dignity than is usual, tall, slender, and of a very fine and graceful figure. He was prematurely gray from ill health. His preaching was Biblical and impressive. He and his wife were companions for more than half a century. Their son, Roswell, educated at Hillsdale College, was a pre-eminent member of the Tennessee bar, but died suddenly in Feb. 1868.

Of their seven children who survived at his death, Benjamin, who died earlier, had served as a member of the Wisconsin Legislature, and for six years as Treasurer of Rock County. His own words, "...about five hundred have received baptism at my hands." He planted twelve churches and assisted in several others. He assisted in ordaining about twenty ministers and preached about six hundred funeral sermons. The denomination lost one of its early pillars, and the church one of its wisest counselors.

Rufus Ellis Cheney
Birth:
May 4, 1780 Hillsborough
County,
New Hampshire
Death:
Aug. 30, 1869
New Berlin,
Waukesha County, Wisconsin
Burial:
Sunnyside Cemetery,
New Berlin,
Waukesha County, Wisconsin

Cheney was born in Antrim, New Hampshire. He began to preach about twenty-three years of age and was ordained in 1810. After residing for a time in Vermont, near St. Johnsbury, he moved to Attica, New York, where, with the assistance of Rev. N. Brown, he was instrumental in gathering a church. During his three years at that place it increased to 120 members. In 1817 he settled in Porter, Ohio, and organized a small church, which soon numbered more than 100. (This church still exists and the pastor is the moderator of the Ohio State Association and active in the national convention.) In his labors the Little Scioto Quarterly Meeting had its origin. Returning to New York, he ministered to the Attica church several years, and built there a house of worship. In 1837 he settled in Wisconsin, where he organized the New Berlin church in 1840, and the Honey Creek church in 1841, -the first churches gathered in the state. He was the father of the Honey Creek Quarterly Meeting, and, with Cary and others, took an important part in building up the Wisconsin Yearly Meeting. He enjoyed the confidence of all who knew him.

Don't worry about tomorrow because God has already taken care of it.

He was an ordained Freewill Baptist minister, and settled in 1848 on a farm in Burnett, (Dodge Co) Wis., where he died. He united with the Rolling Prairie church at its organization; received license to preach in August, 1854, and was ordained by the Waupun Quarterly Meeting, in February, 1858. He was at different time's pastor of some of the churches in the vicinity, and was respected by all.

Good-by; but oh, it is not forever

Joseph Clough
Birth:
Oct. 9, 1813
Gilmanton, Belknap County,
New Hampshire
Death:
Dec. 12, 1894
Burnett, Dodge County,
Wisconsin
Burial:
Hyland Prairie Cemetery
Oak Grove, Dodge County,
Wisconsin

Rev Ruel Cooley
Birth:
Apr. 19, 1819
New York
Death:
Apr. 13, 1885
Johnstown
Rock County

Wisconsin
Burial:
North Johnstown Cemetery
Milton
Rock County
Wisconsin

He graduated from Oberlin College, Ohio, in 1846. Rev. Cooley was an ordained Freewill Baptist minister and pastor. He had also served as missionary to India before his health forced him from the field. He was involved in preaching and organizing churches in the western states, and was about to go to Kenesaw, NE, when he took ill and died.

It was a great loss to the fledging church movement there as he was an able minister and esteemed by all who knew him.

Abner Coombs
Birth:
Dec. 1, 1794
Brunswick, Cumberland County, Maine
Death:
Mar. 15, 1880
Honey Creek, Walworth County, Wisconsin

Burial:
Honey Creek Cemetery
Honey Creek,
Walworth County, Wisconsin
Plot: Block 3 Lot 2

He was converted when twenty-two years of age and married to Annstrus Melcher two years later. His ordination by the Sebec, Quarterly Meeting took place Sept. 22, 1830. Residing at Foxcroft, he organized a church there and at Sangerfield, and assisted in gathering several others. Removing to Wisconsin in 1842, he soon united with the Honey Creek church, and remained in it until his death. He was pastor of that church seven years, also for a time at Pike Grove and Wheatland, Sharon and other places also enjoyed his labors. He baptized 178 converts, was thoroughly evangelical and never swerved from the plain precepts of the Bible.

Albion P. Coombs
Birth:
1829
Death:
Sep. 22, 1899
Burial:
Oakwood Cemetery
Waterford
Racine County
Wisconsin
Plot: Section 51

A Freewill Baptist minister who did good work lbion Paris Coombs was the son of Rev. Abner and Annstrus (Melcher) COOMBS. He was married to Harriet White 5 Oct 1848. His father and mother were living in their HH in their late years.

Isaac G Davis
Birth:
Mar. 18, 1819
Canada
Death:
Dec. 23, 1862
Fayette, Lafayette County,
Wisconsin
Burial:
Fayette Cemetery
Fayette, Lafayette County,
Wisconsin,

His parents were Silas L. Davis and Phoebe (Bennett) DAVIS. His family had moved to Vermont and his brother, Rev. Jairus E. Davis was in a protracted meeting when Isaac G. declared that from 'from that moment on he was for the Lord.' He began to feel it his duty to preach, and in 1838, he began holding meetings and studying with reference to the great work. His efforts were favorably looked on and the Huntington Quarterly Meeting of Freewill Baptist, gave him license in June 1839 to preach. He was ordained the next year on the 26th of Sept. 1840. He was accepted by the Missions Board as a foreign missionary, but it was finally concluded that his health would not endure the climate of India. However, his heart was always enlisted in the cause of Missions, and he gave of his scanty means, as well as his life going and preaching, to help. While attending Biblical School at Lowell, he labored with the church in Roxbury, MA, which was greatly increased in strength and numbers. In Aug. 8, 1843, he was married to Almira Bullock, in Lowell, Mass. They spent one year in Portsmouth, NH, then two years of faithful service to Deerfield, NH. A trip to Nova Scotia and New Brunswick was made where his labors were successful. After a three-month supply of the desk at Lawrence, he removed West. For several years, with the exception of a year or two spent in Elgin, Ill., most of his time was given to missionary labors in Boon and McHenry Quarterly Meetings and in other parts of Illinois and Wisconsin. In 1855, he took the pastoral care of the FWB Church in Fayette, WI, where (with exception of one year in Warren, Ill) he continued faithfully until his death. He enjoyed the confidence of his congregation. In Dec. 1862, he served as moderator in Quarterly Meeting, apparently in good health; was immediately taken ill, and died in eleven days. Prof. Ransom Dunn, whom he had selected, addressed a large and deeply affected audience upon the occasion, from II Corinthians 4:17-18. His life and example were unusually blameless. His friends were many; his enemies, none. He left the inestimable treasure of a good example to the world.He left four brothers,-- Mr. Silas A. Davis, the Yearly Meeting Clerk; Deacon W. Bennet Davis, and Revs. Jairus E. and Kinsman R. Davis. Also, three or four sisters, and an aged father, who, for more than fifty years, has been a faithful member of the Freewill Baptist Denomination. His own family consisted of a daughter and three sons, the oldest of whom went in the army, and the youngest–a child two years old–to heaven, having departed two days in advance of his father. He was aged 43 years. Source: Info is from an old book, "Memoirs of Eminent Preachers in the Freewill Baptist Denomination (1874)," by Selah Hibbard Barrett. (Copyright is public domain). Also, a short bio confirms relationships to his minister brothers, etc, in *Cyclopedia of Free Baptist,* pub. 1889, by Burgess and Ward as well as a short bio of Isaac G. Family.

Samuel Drown
Birth:
Mar. 10, 1796
Sheffield,
Caledonia County, Vermont
Death:
Sep. 9, 1884
Beaver Dam,

Dodge County, Wisconsin
Burial:
Oakwood Cemetery,
Beaver Dam,
Dodge County, Wisconsin,
Plot: Sec 1b

He was ordained a Free Will Baptist minister in 1831 in New Hampshire and labored for a time in the Wheelock Quarterly Meeting, and also, in New Hampshire, where he was a member of the Legislature three years. In 1845. He moved to Dodge Co., Wisconsin, and obtained land, and continued to reside at Beaver Dam until his death. He was treasurer of Dodge Co. in 1847, and connected with the Jefferson QM of FW Baptists, being widely known and respected.

Rev Daniel Wood Edwards
BIRTH
11 Oct 1825
Lebanon, York County,
Maine, USA
DEATH
26 May 1902 (aged 76)
Beloit, Rock County,
Wisconsin, USA
BURIAL
Oakwood Cemetery
Beloit, Rock County,
Wisconsin
PLOT   OP-E-25-4,3

He was the son of James L. and Caroline M. (Wood) Edwards. On September 19, 1861, he married Mrs. Mary Gilman.Receiving education at Geauga Seminary and also Benjamin Stanton's School at West Lebanon, ME, he was ordained Jan. 4, 1852, by the Jackson (Iowa) Q.M. [Quarterly Meeting]. His pastoral work has been with the Chagrin Falls church, Ohio, the Manchester, Caledonia, and Laona churches in Illinois, the Stewart and Shirland churches in Ohio, and at North Marengo, Ill. In one year, he traveled 1200 miles in Wisconsin in evangelist work, and for two years he continued the work in Iowa, traveling on horseback and in buggy with no salary and no collections for himself.

Benjamin Garret Fowler
Birth:
1774
Death:
Dec. 12, 1848
Burial:
Union Cemetery
Brothertown, Calumet
County, Wisconsin

Fowler, a native of Mohegan, Conn., and one of the Brothertown Indians, was ordained in New York in 1819, and died in Manchester, Wis., Dec. 12, 1848, aged 73 years. "This may certify that Benjamin Fowler is acknowledged as a public administrator in the Free-Will Baptist connection.- Done by order of the Union Yearly Meeting Council at Sherbum, June 14, 1845. Samuel Nichols, Yearly Meeting Clerk."

He was much loved as a good citizen and philanthropist and was respected as a faithful minister. In his advanced years he supplied the Manchester church, preaching his last sermon December 2. He was marshal of the town for several years, and a peacemaker from 1808 to 1811. In religious affairs he was a leader, and ministered as an elder of the Freewill Baptist order. He removed to Wisconsin with his family, and aged 74. His gravestone bears the tribute: 'He spoke the language of his Master, 'little children, love one another',

Josiah Fowler
Birth:
Jul. 29, 1794
Thetford,
Orange County, Vermont
Death:
Dec. 29, 1864
Wyocena,
Columbia County, Wisconsin
Burial:
Wyocena Cemetery, yocena,
Columbia County, Wisconsin

His father was a native of England, a cooper by trade and lived in humble circumstances, which compelled the children early to form habits of industry. Rev. Fowler at 13 years of age, gave himself to God; he became connected with the Free Baptists when twenty-one, and while teaching in Camillon, New York, preached his first sermon in his schoolhouse. He received license in Apr 1816, and ordination Aug. 20, 1819, Rev's N. Brown, N. Ketchum and N. Hinckley serving on the council. He had great success as an evangelist and in surrounding towns he baptized multiplied converts which enabled him to organize churches. Out of the many converts, nine became ministers. In 1836, Rev. Fowler became a member of the Ohio and Pennsylvania Y.M., and was active in the work, serving as pastor at Mecca, Ohio. Wellsburgh and Big Bend, Pennsylvania, health permitted. A few months before his death he sought relief in a change of climate, but without avail, and died in Wyocena, Wisconsin. Rev. Fowler was esteemed as one of the church's ablest ministers. He had strong religious sensibilities and was greatly blessed of God in his chosen line of work. Two of his sons served as officers in the Civil War; one became an attorney and one professor of mathematics in Hillsdale College.

Rev Joseph Benjamin Gidney
Birth:
Apr., 1847, Canada
Death: 1933
Wisconsin
Burial:
Milton Cemetery
Milton
Rock County
Wisconsin

Spouse: Annie E Gidney
(1852 - 1914)

Emeline *Wade* Griffin
Birth:
Mar. 29, 1817
Ontario, Canada
Death:
Sep. 1, 1906
Hortonville,
Outagamie County,
Wisconsin
Burial:
Allenville Cemetery,
Allenville,
Winnebago County, isconsin

Married Jacob Griffin 06 Oct. 1836, in Canada. Her husband was a minister, who went from Canada to United States and back, finally to Wisconsin, where they for 35 years together had been successful in their preaching and church endeavors. She, successfully preached alongside her husband, as per written records. Their work resulted in much good. She died at age 89.

Jacob Griffin
Birth:
Nov. 5, 1815
Lincoln County, Ontario, Canada
Death:
Jan. 26, 1901
Hortonville, Outagamie County, Wisconsin
Burial:
Allenville Cemetery, llenville, Winnebago County, Wisconsin

His parents held loyalist sentiments and went to Canada to escape. It was mostly an untamed area, and Jacob did not have many educational opportunities, but at age 16 years, he heard Rev's David Marks and Obadiah Jenkins preach. After the meeting he joined the Free Will Baptist Church there. He began to preach in 1843, and ordained in Canada in 1844. At once he began in evangelizing and organizing churches. On 06 Oct. 1836, he married Emeline WADE, and shortly thereafter, they migrated to Illinois. He was useful there in that state, but moved back to Canada in 1852, remaining until 1867, when he accepted a call to Winnebago and Vineland churches in Wisconsin. He was abundant in his labors, pastoring and evangelizing in the region. Over 700 were baptized by him. He was a sympathetic friend, a true minister, who sought neither wealth nor the praise of men. His wife Emeline survived him; two sons, Rev. Z.F. Griffin of Keuka College, New York, who for ten years was a missionary in India; Norvell W. Griffin, a farmer in Oklahoma. A short funeral service was held at his home, then his body was carried by train to the Free Baptist

Church, in Allenville, where the Rev. J. M. Kayser, long-time friend, and fellow churchman, officiated at his service.(more information can be found on the Wisconsin Free Will Baptist Historical Society web site, History of Nebraska, Vol 3, by Julius S. Morton).

Rev William B Hamlin
Birth:
1816
Vermont
Death:
Aug. 6, 1874
Burial:
Evergreen Cemetery
Oconto
Oconto County
Wisconsin

Nathaniel Harvey
Birth:
Jan. 9, 1788
New Hampshire
Death:
Jun. 4, 1870
Fulton, Rock County,
Wisconsin
Burial:
Mount Pleasant Cemetery
Janesville, Rock County,
Wisconsin

Harvey was born in Nottingham, N. H., and was converted in early life under the labors of Elder Benjamin Randall. He began to preach when eighteen years of age, and was ordained in 1812, when he settled at Atkinson, Maine, where he remained pastor about thirty years. In 1844 he moved to Fulton, Wisconsin, where he remained until about four years before his death, at Evansville. While in Wisconsin, Brother Harvey was connected with the Calvinistic Baptists.

Herman Jenkins
Birth:
1785
Massachusetts
Death:
Jul. 23, 1855
Heart Prairie
Walworth County,Wisconsin
Burial:

Millard Cemetery
Millard
Walworth County,Wisconsin
Plot: Sec. A, Row 4

He was converted in a revival immediately following the organization of the Bethany, NY, church in 1809, about twenty-four years of age. The second session of the Bethany Free Will Baptist Quarterly Meeting (Q.M.) was held at his house in Batavia in May 1813, and he was ordained Aug. 20, 1814. He remained connected with the Bethany church until 1840, when he went to Ashtabula Co. Ohio, and in 1843, he settled in Wisconsin. His death occurred at his house on Heart Prairie, Wis., July 23, 1855.His education was limited, but his acquaintance with human nature and experimental religion, and his great familiarity with the Bible enabled him to labor with great success. The venerable Nathaniel Brown being also with the Bethany church, Bro. Jenkins was permitted to labor much abroad.

His firm health permitted him to indulge his ardent zeal. He was at Boston, NY, in 1817; at Middlebury, NY in 1824, and saw here and elsewhere the abundant blessing of God. He made an exploring tour into

Canada in 1822, assisting Elder Banghart at Dunwich, and another tour in 1828, gathering the church in Southwold. He was especially successful at Trumbull and Hart's Grove, OH. Having preached at Penfield, NY in 1830, a revival began, which was continued by others and over fifty persons dated their conviction to his sermons. Few men on the Western frontier have done more efficient service.

William W Joy
Birth:
Mar. 29, 1831
New York, USA
Death:
Oct. 17, 1906
Wisconsin
Burial:
Mound Cemetery
Racine
Racine County, Wisconsin

William W. Joy, age 30, was a student of Hillsdale College, Hillsdale, Mich, in 1860 Census. He is living in Household of College Prof. Henry S. Whipple, 46y, b. VT, and wife, Elizabeth, 45y, b. MA.A Whipple dau, Roseann, 19, and Marion Packard (female) 18, b NH as well as W.W. JOY, 30, b NY were all college students.

He was mar. To Ruhama Lefler, and they had at least one child, May Joy. Mar. Jerome Spencer, 26 June 1907, Racine, WI.

In 1855 Renselaer Co. NY census Wm. W.'s parents were shown as Martin Joy, age 83y of Renselear Co. NY and Polly Joy, 74ys.

(See Ruhama Joy's memorial for her obit).

J. M. Kayser
Birth:
Mar. 19, 1831 Columbiana
County, Ohio
Death:
Dec. 21, 1913
Seattle,
King County, Washington

Burial:
Allenville Cemetery,
Allenville,
Winnebago County,
Wisconsin

He was ordained a Free Will Baptist minister, in Athens, Ohio Quarterly Meeting in 1862. He had been licensed by same, on Nov. 23, 1861. During his first two years of ministry, he traveled as evangelist with the Rev's I. Z Haning and B. V. Tewksbury. He prepared in the Atwood, Ohio Institute for one year, then finishing with the University of Ohio for three years. His pastorates included: Albany, Ohio; Liberty, Illinois; Gobleville and Waverly, Michigan; and Winneconie, Wisconsin, where his labors were blessed. He has filled the Chair of Mathematics at Atwood Institute for three years; was a delegate to the General Conference, was president of the Wisconsin Home Mission Board. He also served in Nebraska Free Will Baptist churches doing mission work and helping there, before going to Wisconsin, where he spent 36 years of his ministry. He was used in many funerals and weddings as he ministered in Wisconsin.

Rev Phipps Waldo Lake
BIRTH
1 May 1789
Albany County, New York,
USA
DEATH
17 Aug 1860 (aged 71)
Walworth, Walworth County,
Wisconsin, USA
BURIAL
Brick Church Cemetery
Walworth, Walworth County,
Wisconsin
PLOT Section 1, Row 16,
Stone 1

Phipps Waldo Lake was an American politician and Baptist clergyman. Born in Hoosick, New York, Lake served in the United States Army during the War of 1812 was in the battle at Sacketts Harbor, New York. Lake was a minister in the Free Will Baptist Church and preached in Cortland and Montgomery Counties, New York. He lived in Ames, New York where he preached for fourteen years. In 1839, Lake moved to Big Foot, Wisconsin Territory in the town of Walworth. He farmed and was the Baptist minister of a church in Lake Geneva, Wisconsin. In 1854, Lake served in the Wisconsin State Assembly as a Whig and later joined the Republican Party. Notes: 'History of Walworth County, Wisconsin,' vol. II, Albert Clayton Beckwith, B.F. Bowen & Company, Indianapolis, Indiana: 1912, Biographical Sketch of Phipps Waldo Lake, pg. 936-938

Rev Leman W Lee
Birth:
Aug. 3, 1784
Vermont
Death:
Feb. 15, 1875
Winnebago County

Wisconsin
Burial:
Allenville Cemetery
Allenville
Winnebago County
Wisconsin
Plot: Section A, Row 3

Rev. Lemon W. LEE, a native of Vermont, was licensed to preach in 1820 and ordained in Boston, N.Y., Nov. 12, 1831. He labored several years in western New York and saw much good.

After a season in Illinois, he went, some twenty years before his death, to Wisconsin, laboring for a time at Winneconne, and later residing at Winnebago, where he died, aged 90 years.

His last sermon was preached the June preceding his death. He was a true, devoted minister.

Greenly Mevis
Birth:
Aug. 6, 1818
New York
Death:
Aug. 21, 1894
Waukesha
Waukesha County
Wisconsin

Burial:
Prairie Home Cemetery
Waukesha
Waukesha County,Wisconsin
Plot: Sec N, Blk 50, Lot 1, Sp 1
Greenly Mevis wrote many religious pamphlets. He was married to: Orinda H Mevis (1831 - 1898) and to Caroline Janes Mevis (1823 - 1887)*

William Mitchell
Birth:
Mar. 5, 1821
Death:
Jan. 8, 1904
Burial:
Union Cemetery
Hortonville, Outagamie
County, Wisconsin

Rev. William Mitchell was born at New Portland, Maine and married to R.C. Staples in 1847. Twenty-seven years later [1874] he was married again to B.L. Raymond. He was converted in 1840 and ordained in 1844. His ministry of more than forty years has been spent mostly in Wisconsin with the Fairwater, Harrisville, Rosendale, Eldorado, Greenbush, South Prairie, Winnebago, Vinland, Hortonville and Dale churches. The church at Hortonville, where he served as pastor at intervals, in all amounting to more than twenty years.

Elder David Moon
Birth:
Jan. 19, 1803
Herkimer County
New York
Death:
Dec. 8, 1877
Dodge County
Wisconsin
Burial:
Kekoskee Cemetery

Kekoskee
Dodge County, Wisconsin

Son of Benajah and Sarah Gould Silver Moon. David and Catherine's children: Priscilla (Fleming), Emma (Crane), Owen S., Esther Catherine (Roby), William, Henry, Prudence, Clarissa (Clark), Albert, Charles, David Jr., and Tryphena.

The 1860 census enumerates him as a farmer.

The 1870 census enumerates him as a clergyman.

--From the 110th anniversary booklet of the Russia (NY) Union church:

-David, born Jan. 19, 1803; died Dec. 8, 1877, in Williamstown, Dodge County, Wis.; married, 1st, Catherine Rhodes, born Nov. 30, 1802, the daughter of Richard and Effy (Clapper) Rhodes; 2nd, Martha Kinney of Mohawk, N.Y.; 3rd, Maranda Nobles. David Moon was a Baptist clergyman and served the Russia Church, 1847 to 1848. Elder David Moon, as he was called, went to California alone, stayed four years and returned with a bag of gold which he sold for $1200. He then went to Wisconsin and purchased a farm. He lived at

Kekoskee, Wis., and later Williamstown, Wis.

Inscription:

In the circle at top: Absent Not Dead/ Christ Is My Hope. The bottom inscription-very worn-I think the second line starts with "Was" and ends with "death", the third line seems to be "have laid his body in this grave" and the last line" His Soul Has Gone to Rest".

Rev Joseph Baker Morford
Birth:
Nov., 1795
Death:
May, 1855
Burial:
Pierceville Cemetery
Sun Prairie
Dane County, Wisconsin

Early FW Baptist preacher in Wisconsin.

Augustus Phillips
Birth:
Mar. 27, 1825
Marcellus,
New York
Death:
Apr. 30, 1907
Eau Claire,
Wisconsin
Burial:
South Lawrence Cemetery
De Pere,
Brown County,
Wisconsin

The first two decades of Wrightstown's Freewill Baptist congregation are inexorably tied to the career of Augustus Phillips, one of northeastern Wisconsin's most remarkable religious figures in the second half of the nineteenth century. Three of Phillips' five brothers became Freewill Baptist ministers serving congregations in New England. Phillips apparently received no formal education.

He left home at the age of eleven and went to Ohio, then back to New York, and then to Rhode Island, working as a farm laborer and woolen goods manufacturer. In 1846 he married Minerva Greene, and in 1851 the couple moved to Wisconsin, where he purchased 160 acres of land in an unincorporated settle- ment known as Sniderville, approximately 2 miles northwest of the village of Wrightstown. This farm, later expanded with the purchase of additional acreage, was the family's home for the next 54 years. In September 1864 Phillips enlisted in Company E of Wisconsin's 42nd Infantry Regiment; he was mustered out in June 1865, after distinguished service, with the rank of corporal. Phillips' religious activities began soon after he arrived in Wisconsin.

He served as a lay preacher beginning in the mid-1850s at the "earnest request" of his neighbors, preaching to Methodist congregations, a practice he may have continued for ten years. He was ordained a Freewill Baptist minister in 1866.

On January 6, 1866, Phillips and fourteen men and women met and organized Wrightstown's Freewill Baptist congregation. Two years later they acquired land and began constructing their church in the village. Within a few years, some of the original members organized separate Freewill Baptist congregations at Sniderville and at Greenleaf, another unincorporated settlement approximately four miles east of Wrightstown. Phillips is credited with establishing all three of these congregations, and he served all three as pastor until 1885. In that year he withdrew from the pastorates of Wrightstown and Greenleaf but continued as pastor at Sniderville, finally retiring from that pulpit in 1905.

Phillips was known for leading successful revivals throughout his pastorate. In September 1876 a revival began in Wrightstown "which bids fair to be equal to the one recently held over at

Greenleaf, where between 40 and 50 conversions.

In addition to preaching in the three churches at Wrightstown, Greenleaf, and Sniderville, Phillips also exchanged pulpits with other Freewill Baptist ministers throughout the region, including Kaukauna, Oshkosh, Shiocton, and Hortonville, preaching to the latter congregation every other week "for quite a long time. Phillips and lay members of the Wrightstown church also attended Quarterly Meetings of the Waupun District at various communities throughout northeastern Wisconsin. In October 1905 Phillips preached his farewell sermon to the Sniderville Baptist congregation; Baptists from Wrightstown, Kaukauna, Appleton "and other places" attended. Phillips died in Eau Claire. His body was returned to northeastern Wisconsin by train, his funeral "very largely attended, people from Menasha, Greenleaf, Kaukauna, Wrightstown and De Pere being present." Phillips was buried in the Sniderville Baptist cemetery. Phillips' wife Minerva died on January 6, 1913, and is buried next to him in the Sniderville cemetery-the South Lawrence Cemetery.

Mowry Phillips
Birth:
Mar. 16, 1857
Death:
Jan. 27, 1942
Burial:
South Lawrence Cemetery
De Pere, Brown County,
Wisconsin

Parents: Augustus Phillips (1825 – 1907) Minerva A. Greene Phillips (1825 – 1913)

Rev Mary Pitcher
Birth:
May 2, 1887
Death: unknown
Burial:
Colby Cemetery, Colby
Clark County,
Wisconsin

PITCHER, Rev. Mrs. Mary; (May or may not be, but she was a minister in Wis); Bur. beside husband, Benj. Pitcher; Pitcher, Mary (1832 - 1887), Taylor County, Wisconsin Biographical, History & Ancestry Records
Pitcher, Mary (1832 - 1887), Taylor County, Wisconsin Biographical, History & Ancestry Records
Pitcher, Mary (1832 - 1887), Taylor County, Wisconsin Biographical Records

James Raymar Pope
Birth:
May 13, 1819
Windsor
Hartford County, Connecticut
Death:
Jun. 8, 1897
Clinton,Rock County,
isconsin
Burial:
Clinton Cemetery
Clinton,Rock County,
Wisconsin

Rev. James Raymar Pope 9th child of Dr. Samuel Pope and Freelove Waterman Pope of Union, Broome Co., NY., and Freelove Pope of Janesville, Rock Co., WI.At the age of 5 years his father Samuel Pope, was a prominent physician, moved to Broome Co., NY. At the age of fifteen James' father died, leaving a family of nine children, of which he was the seventh son. In 1839 Mr. Pope came to Wisconsin probably with mother and brother Cyrus Waterman Pope, settling in Rock County, near Janesville where other brother Virgil Pope resided Section 14, Janesville. At the age of twenty-two he began the study of law, but was converted a year later and joined the Free Will Baptist Church. He abandon the bar and took the pulpit, and began preparation for the same at once. In June 1848 Bro. Pope was ordained to the gospel ministry and in 12 June 1851 in Harmony, Rock Co., WI., was united in marriage to Justina V. Miller a daughter of Cornelius Miller and wife Selinda Smith Miller.In 1889 he was pastor of Longbranch Free Will Baptist Church, located 6 miles southeast of Tecumseh, Johnson Co., Nebraska.

W. A. Potter
Birth:
Jan. 23, 1820
Bennington, Vermont
Death:
Jul. 23, 1880
Monticello, Wisconsin
Burial:
Zwingli Cemetery
Monticello
Green County, Wisconsin

Rev Oscar J Shannon
Birth:
Aug. 5, 1842
Vermont
Death:
Apr. 9, 1878
Kansas
Burial:
Burnett Corners Cemetery
Burnett
Dodge County,Wisconsin

SHANNON, Rev. Oscar J), mar. 7 July 1870 to Gertrude Mary Lockwood, Dodge Co. Wis; Fth/Mth: John A Shannon and Maryette/Margarette (?)
Inscription:
Age 35y 8m 4d

Rev Robert Davenport
Sparks
Birth: Feb. 8, 1827
Summit
Schoharie County
New York
Death: Jan. 7, 1913
Waushara County
Wisconsin

Burial:
Plainfield Cemetery
Plainfield
Waushara County
Wisconsin
Plot: Row 1, Lot 25,

SPARKS, Rev. R. D (Robt. Davenport), 1827-1913, Bur. Plainfield   Cem.,Plainfield, Waushara   Co.   Wis.   His memorial/stone has "Rev" and   Kevin   Sparks   is   the contributor.
Robert Davenport Sparks is my 4th great Uncle. Yes he was a Free Baptist Minister. He retired in 1907. I have virtual   cemeteries   on   my profile listing some of the marriages he performed.

A. B. Taylor
Birth:
Unknown
Southwold, Ontario, Canada
Death:
Jan. 28, 1876
Burial:
Rienzi Cemetery,
Fond du Lac,
Fond du Lac County,
Wisconsin

Rev. Taylor, when nineteen years of age, became a follower of the Saviour, and soon after began preaching. During his labors in Canada he was permitted to see the results of his efforts, and conversions among those with whom he toiled were of frequent occurrence. But as a sense of the paramount importance of the work in which he was engaged came to be fully recognized by him, he felt the need of greater educational advantages than he had yet enjoyed accordingly and soon after entered the Theological department of Hillsdale College. During the time he spent here he was continually at work for the Master, usually preaching three times upon the Sabbath. Revivals seemed to be a natural outgrowth of his labors, and he was permitted to be largely instrumental in the organizing of two or more churches in southern Michigan. So zealously did he labor that it was said of him by one of the teachers, "He has done a lifework before his graduation. "Completing his studies in June, 1873, he received a call to the pastorate of the Free Baptist church in Fond du Lac, and soon after entered upon his work. There he continued to labor until a few weeks before his death.

George A. Taylor
Birth:
Nov. 13, 1842
Huntington
Huntington County, Indiana
Death:
Jun. 29, 1913
Los Angeles
Los Angeles County,
California
Burial:
Greenwood Cemetery
Dallas
Barron County, Wisconsin

He died at the Pacific Branch, National Home for Disabled Veteran Soldiers, Los Angeles County, California, aged 70 years, 7 months and 16 days, where he had been admitted November 7, 1912. His remains were shipped to Dallas, Barron County, Wisconsin, and buried there beside the remains of his wife Nancy in Greenwood Cemetery.On November 24, 1859, George was united in marriage to Nancy Alvise Rogers, by Reverend G. Dissmore, at Lindina, Juneau County, Wisconsin. Nancy was born August 17, 1838, in Indiana. She died December 29, 1905, aged 67 years, 4 months and 12 days, and was buried in the Taylor family plot in Greenwood Cemetery. They were the parents of nine children. George was a Civil War veteran who enlisted

March 10, 1865, at St. Paul, Minnesota, to serve one year as a Private in the 1st Minnesota Infantry, and was mustered into Federal service with Company C the next day at the same location. At that time he received 1/3 of his $100.00 enlistment bounty and was listed as a 22 year and 3 month old, 5'8" tall farmer, with brown hair, brown eyes and a fair complexion, born in Huntington, Indiana, and from Mapleton, Cottonwood Township, Brown County, Minnesota. On March 5, 1865, his name was on a roll of men at the Draft Rendezvouz at Ft. Snelling, St. Paul, Minnesota. On July 14, 1865, George was discharged with Company C, at Jeffersonville, Indiana. His original discharge is in his pension file at the National Archives. On their muster out roll it was noted that he was due 1/3 of his enlistment bounty less $6.00 for arms retained.After his discharge, George returned to Minnesota. He was ordained by the Blue Earth Valley Quarter Meeting in Minnesota, June 13, 1869. He assisted in the organization of the Medo, Minnesota and Dallas, Wisconsin churches and was formerly clerk of the Blue Earth Valley Quarterly Meeting. He was also the first clerk of the Minnesota Southern Yearly Meeting, was a clerk of the St. Croix Quarter Meeting, and was a member of the Minnesota yearly Meeting Home Mission Board. As a citizen he held the office of accessor, town clerk, chairman of the Board Of Supervisors, Justice of the Peace, member of the school board.

He resided there until 1870, when he moved to Mauston, Juneau County, Wisconsin. In 1871, he moved to Colby, Clark County, Wisconsin, and in 1875, to Huntington, Huntington County, Indiana, returning the same year to Mauston. In 1876, he moved to Dallas, Barron County, Wisconsin. He farmed near Dallas and Hillsdale, in that county, and nearby Ridgeland, Dunn County, Wisconsin, until 1908, when he moved to Cauldwell, Idaho. In 1912 he moved to Los Angeles County, California.

Rev George W. Town
Birth: 1810
Vermont
Death: 1894
Burial:
Oak Center Cemetery
Oak Center
Fond du Lac County
Wisconsin

His memorial already had "Rev" on it. He mar. Sophia Jane (Blackwood), and they had at least nine or ten children. I've found several and sent links. to the parents. He was bn. VT, and was in Clinton Co. NY in 1850, with five kids before ending up in Wisconsin. He had a son, George W. but I have not found anything of him being a minister. He mar. Marcia (Mary) Kising in Wis, 09 July 1874.

Clyde Wayne Tripp
Birth: Apr. 10, 1898
Sparta
Monroe County
Wisconsin
Death: Jan. 7, 1988
New Richmond
St. Croix County
Wisconsin
Burial:
Calvary Cemetery
Deer Park
St. Croix County
Wisconsin

Husband of Eve Bader Tripp and father of Robert, Raymond and Lois. Kind and gentle man. Raised a wonderful family and was a devoted and loving husband. Rev. C. W. (Clyde Wayne); b. 10 April 1898; d. 07 Jan 1988, St. Croix, Wis;

Orin Haines True
Birth:
May 30, 1831
Moultonborough,
Carroll County,
New Hampshire
Death:
Nov. 27, 1913
Burial:
Maple Hill Cemetery
Evansville, Rock County,
Wisconsin
Plot: Original Block 1, Lot 135

His parents, Asa W. and Rebecca (Haines) TRUE, gave him early instruction in religion and he was converted when about five years of age. He graduated from the literary department of the New Hampton Institution in 1858, and subsequently from the theological.

He married Miss Sarah L. Bean, of Candia, NH, on Aug. 22, 1860 and after her death, fourteen years later, he married Mrs. E. H. Hudson, of Johnstown, Wis. His ordination took place June 20, 1861, his subsequent ministry being with the churches at Lisbon and W. Lebanon, ME, N. Scituate, R.I., Nekimi, Rosendale, Fond du Lac, Evansville, Oakland, York Prairie, Monticello, Scott, Marcellon and Winneconne, Wisconsin. Much of the time his pastoral care has been bestowed upon two of these churches simultaneously. Revivals have attended his ministry, and the churches have been strengthened.

Amos Tyler
Birth:
Apr. 11, 1802
Piermont, N. H.
Death:
Aug. 13, 1876
Big Spring, Wis.
Burial:
Big Spring Cemetery
Big Spring, Adams County,
Wisconsin

Tyler died at age 74 years. His early ministry as a licentiate was with the Methodists. In 1834 he moved to Hatley, Québec, Canada, where he united with the Free Baptists, and was ordained Oct. 2I, 1836. Here he preached in various townships until 1855, when his health became impaired and he moved to Newport,Wis. With returning health he again engaged in ministerial work, gathered the Big Spring and Kilbourn City church, and engaged in many revivals in the Sauk County Q. M. He was eminently social, very helpful in prayer and exhortation, and benevolent in his gifts, especially to the needy interestnear his home. His daughter is Mrs. Rev. W. E. Dennett.

Rev Simmons E Very
Birth:
Jun. 16, 1847
New York
Death:
Jul., 1925
Oshkosh
Winnebago County
Wisconsin
Burial:
Riverside Cemetery
Oshkosh
Winnebago County
Wisconsin

He married Viola Eliza Bowen, dau of Elias Bowen and Lucinda (Clark) Bowen, 06 July 1873, Ellicott, Chautauqua Co. NY.He was enum. in 1860, 1870, & 1880 censuses, E. Otto, Cattaraugus Co., NY. In 1900, he was in Illinois. Sometime between 1900-1920, He moved to Wisconsin. The Oshkosh, Wis, City Directories, 1822-1995, shows "Residence: 'Rev. Simmons E. Very, Clergyman.'"
He and Viola had five children, and an obit is included in the memorial of daughter, Letha (Very) Corbett, who d. in 1927.
From State records found on Family Tree(s): Marriage: Viola Eliza Bowen, 06 JUL 1873 in Ellicott, Chautauqua Co., NY
Children:

J. J. Wakefield
Birth:
Sep. 15, 1821
Death:
Jul. 28, 1865
Burial:
Beaver Dam City Cemetery
Beaver Dam, Dodge County,
Wisconsin
Plot: L-29

Wakefield was a native of Cornish, Me., died at age 33 years. Such was the type of his piety that the church urged upon him a license to preach, and he was ordained May 30, 1853, at Neenah, Wisconsin. He preached to destitute churches for a time and in 1854 became pastor of the Berlin and Fairwater churches. After four years he settled with the Johnstown church; but in 1860 he moved his family to La Crosse and traveled for his health yet continued to work for the Master. His gifts were admirably adapted to winning souls, and his early death was widely lamented. Recorded in the *Morning Star* on September 6, 1865.

Babcock Waller
Birth:
Jul. 24, 1813
Washington County,
New York
Death:
Feb. 23, 1891
Fond du Lac County,
Wisconsin
Burial:
Oak Center Cemetery,
Fond du Lac County,
Wisconsin

He became a minister just prior to his marriage. And was among the first to pioneer Freewill Baptist work in Wisconsin. He married Nancy Batchelder in 1832 in New York. They moved to Ohio where he was involved in the ministry until 1842 when he removed to Trenton, Washington County, Wisconsin. A little later he moved back and forth serving both the Trenton Freewill Church and one in Scott, Scheboygen County, Wisconsin. Grieved by the loss of his son, David (Co. D 12th Wisconsin Infantry) a prisoner in Andersonville, he decided that a change was in order, so he moved to Fond du Lac County. He did continue to preach and gave his last sermon in the Boltonville Freewill Baptist Church in the fall of 1890.

School 1843-45. He sought improved health in the West, where he taught schoolHe was ordained by the Fond du Lac Quarterly Meeting, Wisconsin, June 6, 1852. The next August he became pastor of the Boston, New York, church and later of the Attica church. But health failing, he returned to Greenbush, Wis., where he died in the 39th year of his age.He possessed a mind of high order and was an able minister. Inscription:Aged 38 years.

Peter Warren
Birth:
Jan., 1818
Maine
Death:
Mar. 10, 1856
Burial:
Woodland Cemetery
Kohler
Sheboygan County,
Wisconsin

Rev. Peter Warren was converted at the age of sixteen and soon began preparation for the ministry. He graduated at Redfield, Maine, and was in the Biblical

William Warner
Birth:
October 25, 1796
England
Death:
Dec. 3, 1885
Wisconsin
Burial:
Oaks Cemetery
Valton Sauk County,
Wisconsin

He fought in the British ranks at the battle of Waterloo.

After coming to America, he enlisted in the Army of Jesus Christ in 1820 and soon received license to preach. His early labors were in Quebec, Canada and his ordination being received at Hadley, Quebec, Canada on January 17, 1837. Continuing in the Canadian Province most of the time until about 1848 when he moved to Enfield, New Hampshire and labored there and in the vicinity of a number of years. He then moved to New Hampton and while there gave a very able lecture on the Battle of Waterloo. About 1864 he moved to Clementsville21, Wisconsin uniting with the Vineland church.

Rev Francis M. Washburn
Birth:
Aug., 1845
Montgomery County
Indiana
Death:
Dec. 2, 1919
Stanislaus County
California
Burial:
Maple Hill Cemetery
Evansville
Rock County
Wisconsin
Plot: Original Block 2, Lot 19

Rev. F. M. Washburn became connected with the Sauk County Quarterly Meeting (QM), Wisconsin, as early as 1879. He soon became pastor of the Evansville and Oregon churches of the Rock and Dane Q.M., and about 1884 of the Mt. Pleasant church of the Honey Creek QM. His labors in Wisconsin have been highly esteemed. He served for some time as treasurer of the Mission Board and was a delegate to the General Conference in 1886. In 1888 he took charge of the important church at San Francisco, CA

Rev. F.M. Washburn was a Free Will Baptist clergyman, before he became a Methodist, pastoring churches in Wisconsin.

The northern Freewill Baptists merged their churches with the Northern Baptists, or, now, American

Baptists, in 1911. Many of the Free Baptist ministers then went to the Methodists, rather than the Northern Baptists.

Hiram Watrus
Birth:
Jan. 26, 1815
Williamson
Wayne County, New York
Death:
Jan. 25, 1874
Boscobel
Grant County, Wisconsin
Burial:
Boscobel Cemetery
Boscobel
Grant County, Wisconsin

He was converted in 1833, while living in Geneva, Ohio, and ordained in 1861. While at Scott, Wis. He engaged actively in the work of the ministry in Crawford and Grant Counties, residing ten years at Marion and in 1873 went to Boscobel, where he hired a house of worship and soon organized a church. He

was rich in all the Christian graces, and his death was felt to be a great loss.

Rev Emmonds H. Webster
Birth:
Aug. 8, 1830
Onondaga County
New York
Death:
Apr. 28, 1896
Plymouth
Sheboygan County
Wisconsin
Burial:
Union Cemetery
Plymouth
Sheboygan County
Wisconsin

Plymouth Review
Wednesday April 29, 1896
REV E.H. WEBSTER DEAD
He Had Been a Plymouth Resident for the Past Three Years. Was a Baptist Minister and About Ten Years of His

Life Were Devoted to Church Work – He Was a Soldier of the Rebellion, Having Served His Country From '61 to '65 – H.P. Davidson Post G.A.R. to Take Charge of the Funeral.

The death of Rev. Emmonds H. Webster occurred about 9:15 o'clock last evening at his home on South street where he had resided the past three years. He had been in ill health for a number of years and for the past two or three months was confined to his bed a greater share of the time. Although a resident of Plymouth but a comparatively short time he was well known, having resided in the county for a least thirty years, and in his death the city loses one of its most highly respected citizens.

On December 25th, 1857, he was married to Miss Lucy A. Stewart at Sheboygan Falls, and she survives him, besides whom there are four children, Miss Clara Webster, at home, Mrs. O.W. Williams of Ashland, Wis., Clinton of Kaukauna and Lee at home, also an only sister, Mrs. Hiram Ashcraft of Sheboygan Falls.

For four years Mr. Webster served as a soldier in the rebellion, having entered the service Sept. 25, 1861, as a member of Company B., 8th Wisconsin Regiment, and was discharged in 1865. At the close of the war he returned to Greenbush. In 1860 he was ordained a minister of the Baptist church and two years later removed to Boltonville, Washington county, where he continued to preach until 1893. Then account of failing health he was obliged to give up the work, and came to Plymouth where he has since made it his home. Being a member of the H.P. Davidson Post, G.A.R., that order will have charge of the funeral which will be held at one o'clock Thursday afternoon. Rev. Wellman of Greenbush will conduct the services and interment will be made in the city cemetery.

Rev Zere Lysander Wellman
Birth:
Nov. 9, 1835
Otsego County
New York
Death:
Dec. 14, 1908
Dane County
Wisconsin
Burial:
Riverside Cemetery
Stoughton
Dane County
Wisconsin

Son of Buri and Samantha (Sharp) Wellman, husband of Susie Tibbits and father of Edward, Samantha, Ada and Grace.

VETERAN CLERGYMAN GOES TO HIS REWARD

Mr. Wellman's death occurred in M.V. Gunsolus' house on W. Main street, where he and his wife were residing for the winter in order to enable their daughter, Grace, to attend the high school. He was down town Saturday, and was in his usual health until about 8 o'clock in the evening when as before stated, he was taken with a chill.

Funeral services were conducted by Rev. T. B. Hughes at the First Baptist church, Decedent was a native of Otsego County, N.Y., where he was born Nov. 9th, 1835, thus being just past seventy-three years of age. During the Civil war he served three years with the 37th N.Y. Volunteers, and in 1868 came to this locality where he was married two years later to Miss Susan Tibbit. For three years and a half he was pastor of the Star church in Rutland, and afterwards held the pastorate of a Free Baptist church at Greenbush in Sheboygan county, for a period of eight years. He has not now been actively engaged in preaching for many years, residing on his little tract of land a mile south of the Star church.

Rev John Westlake
Birth:
Jan. 5, 1840
Hartland
Devon, England
Death:
Feb. 27, 1902
Winnebago County
Wisconsin
Burial:
Greenbush Cemetery
Greenbush
Sheboygan County
Wisconsin

Born in England, Rev. John Westlake, was the son of Robert and Elizabeth (Hartop) WESTLAKE.

He immigrated to U.S. in 1853. He married Harriet L. (Gibson), dau of Daniel and Dolly Gibson, in Wisconsin, Nov. 01, 1861. His parents lived in Marquette as did Harriett.

Early Freewill Bapt. minister in Wisconsin. Soon after in 1861, he received ordination from the Wolf River Freewill Bapt. Quarterly Meeting and had charge of Harrisville, Greenbury and Raymond Wis. churches. He also held the office of town treasurer.

Jacob Wescher
Birth:
Ger.
Apr. 20, 1847
Death:
Mar. 15, 1904
Burial:
Forest Home Cemetery
Marinette
Marinette County
Wisconsin

His wife was Louise J (Hesse) Wescher, b. Ger, 1858, d. Aug. 1922, and her stone on other side of his obelisk one

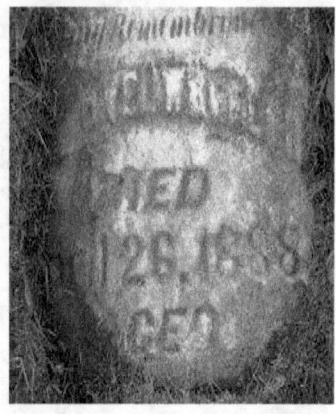

Rev Lovell Wheeler
Birth:
Apr. 24, 1800
Newport, Sullivan County
New Hampshire
Death:
Apr. 26, 1888
Oshkosh
Winnebago CountyWisconsin
Burial:
Ellenwood Cemetery
Oshkosh
Winnebago County
Wisconsin
Plot: Sec F Row 7

.

A faithful minister in the Freewill Baptist church from Newport, N.H. Son of Abel and Prudence(Warren) Wheeler, both of NH. His education was obtained in the academy of his native town, and he was ordained by the ministers of the Weare Quarterly Meeting in August 1831. His ministry was spent in New Hampshire, Vermont, Minnesota and Wisconsin. Several churches were gathered through his labors. They had at least one son, Darius G. Wheeler, b. NH, and mar. Levina Jane Dunn, of Spring Grove, WI, on July 03, 1887, at Albany, Green Co. WI. She was the dau of Wm. Brown, and Lucy (Smily) Brown.

Rev Warren Whiting
Birth:
Oct. 2, 1816
Douglas
Worcester County
Massachusetts
Death:
Jan. 2, 1897
Waupun
Fond du Lac County
Wisconsin
Burial:
Wedges Prairie Cemetery
Waupun
Fond du Lac County
Wisconsin

Warren Whiting was the son of Amos and Alcy (Chase) Whiting. After leaving his parents' home in Mass., he immigrated to Wisconsin, in 1846, first settling in Rock County. He removed to Fond du Lac County a few months later where he engaged in farming, eventually amassing 600 acres of land which he farmed and managed.

At the age of 26, Warren Whiting entered the ministry of the Free-will Baptist Church, and after preaching for a short time was ordained. He continued his ministry for 35 years, but, because of ill health, was forced to lay aside his ministerial duties.

He married (1) Lorinda Keith January 5, 1839, daughter of Lincoln and Submit Keith. He married (2) Ellen C. Ross-Norstraint. She died five months after her marriage to Warren Whiting, her second marriage. He married (3) Ellen O'Harrow. It is possible that Warren Whiting was married a fourth time.

Records of the Fairwater Free-will Baptist Church, Fond du Lac County, show that Rev. Warren Whiting was the second pastor, serving from 1852-1855. The church was organized Feb. 2, 1850 and met in the homes of parishioners. Work began on a church building March 4,

1855 and the new church was dedicated July 10, 1856. Fairwater Free Baptist Church Historical Sketch.